I0236374

A day in the sky

Manja Maas
Lisa Wiersma

Written by:
Manja Maas

Illustrated by:
Lisa Wiersma

Published by:
Graviant Publishers, Doetinchem,
The Netherlands

© August 2017

This work is copyrighted.
All rights reserved by Graviant educational publications, Doetinchem,
The Netherlands, telephone 0031314345400.
No part of this publication may be reproduced, stored in a retrieval system or
transmitted in any other form or by any other means, electronic, mechanical,
photocopying, recording or otherwise without the prior written permission of the
publisher.

ISBN 978-9492593108

Although this book is compiled with care, neither the authors nor the publisher
accepts any liability for the fact that the use of what is offered does not meet the
needs or expectations of the end user, nor for any errors or omissions.

Preface

Octopus loves pushing his boundaries, but this time he goes farther than ever. He decides to go flying!
Lucky for Octopus, his friend Bird is there to help him make his dream come true.

'A Day in the Sky' is about being true to yourself and having faith in yourself.
You can achieve anything you want even when everybody says it's impossible and that you won't succeed.

When Octopus woke up, he had a great idea:
'Today I'm going to fly, does anybody want to join me?'

'But that's impossible,' Shrimp said, 'and why,
would a marine animal go up, all the way to the sky?'
'We were born in the sea,
we belong here you and me.'
'And besides, neither you nor I,
have learned to fly!'

'Well, my friend, I definitely don't agree.'
'We can do anything we want, don't you see!'
'Last time, I ran up a mountain,
my legs hurt a little, but I got it done.'
'That whole experience,
made a complete difference.'

'One day I'll fly!,' to myself I said.
'And whoever doesn't believe me is a feather head.'
'So don't think that I'm lying,
when I say today I'm flying.'

Shrimp said: 'You fly by the seat of your pants!'
'But I think you have a chance.'
'I hope your dream comes true,
break a leg, you have a few.'
'I am just a bit worried, you see,
I want you back here safe with me.'

'I'll be alright, Shrimp, please don't be tense,
this lofty adventure must commence.'
'I stand strongly for what I believe,
I'm sorry if you're worried, but I have to achieve.'
'The problem is you're not the first one,
to say this can't be done.'

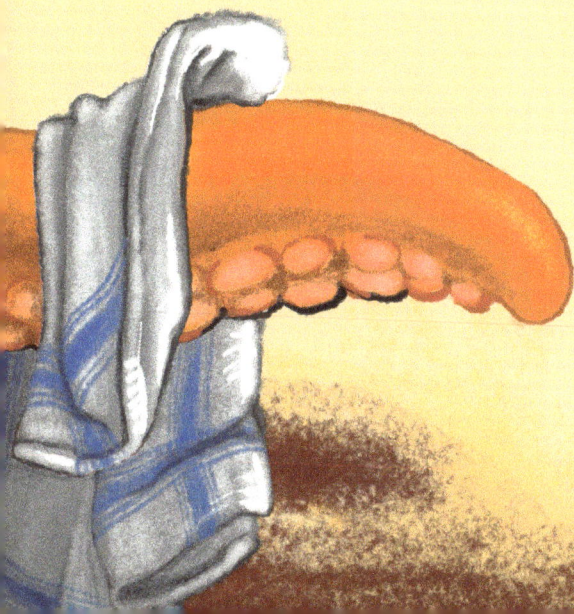

'You're my best friend, you know,
but that doesn't mean though,
that you and me,
can't see things differently.'

'I hope you also see it that way,
and that you're not offended by
what I had to say.'

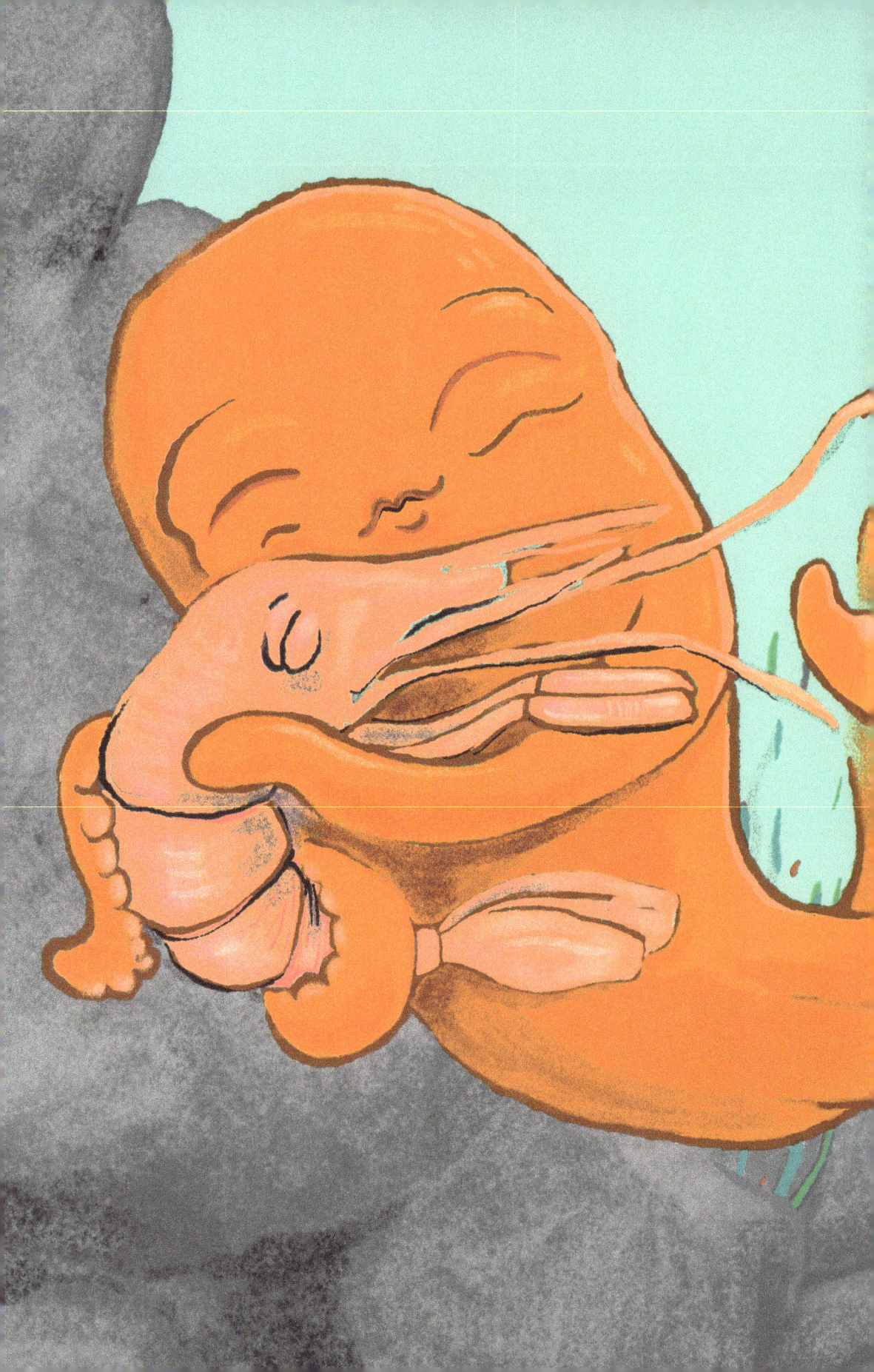

'Have fun Octopus,' Shrimp said,
'and be careful up in the sky.'
'Now give me a kiss and go fly.'

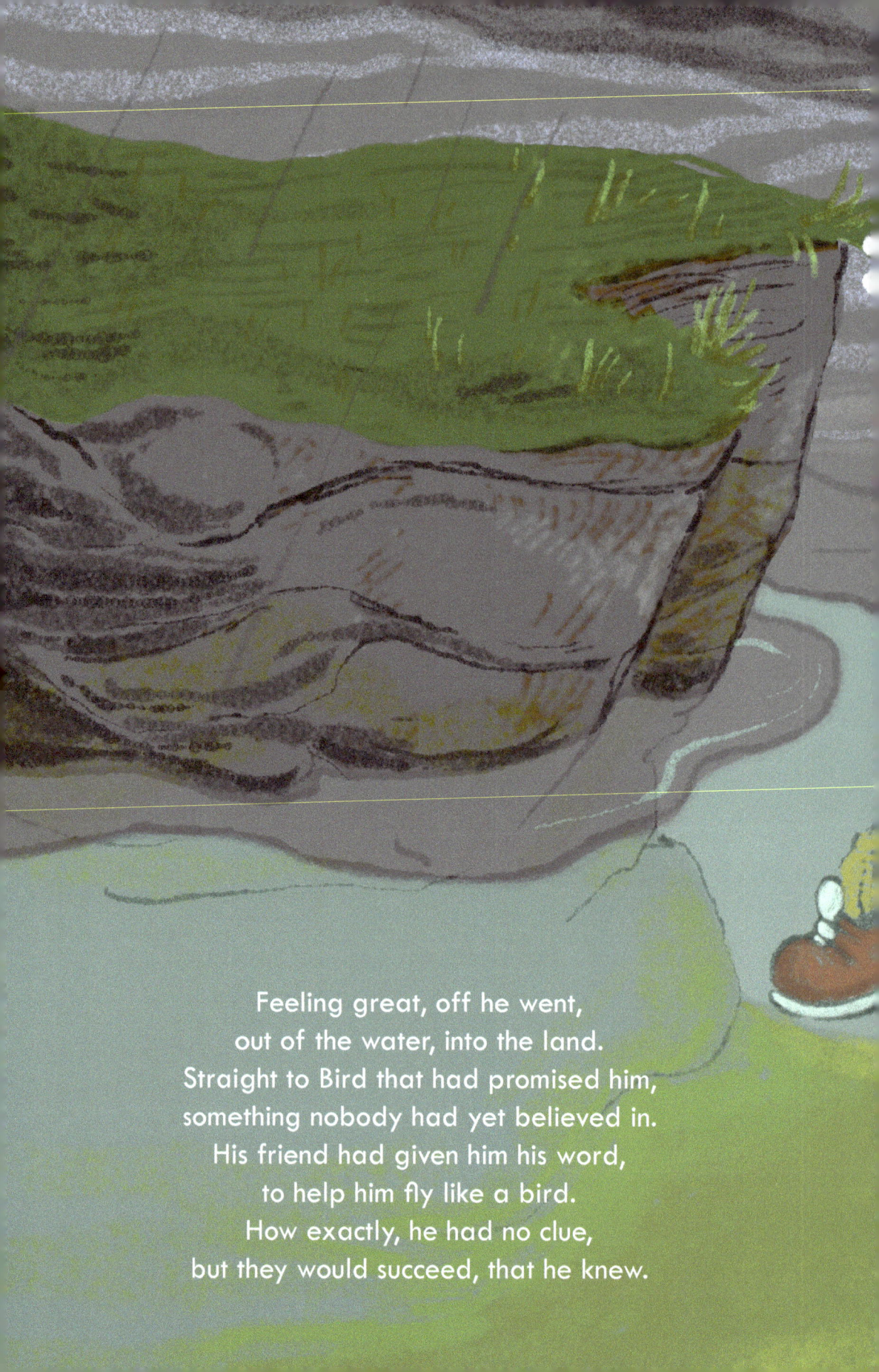

Feeling great, off he went,
out of the water, into the land.
Straight to Bird that had promised him,
something nobody had yet believed in.
His friend had given him his word,
to help him fly like a bird.
How exactly, he had no clue,
but they would succeed, that he knew.

'Hi Octopus', Bird said. 'The weather isn't nice, I say.'
'But when you can fly, bad weather can never ruin your day.'
'Dark clouds may appear at first sight,
an obstacle on the way to the bright light.'
'But when down low it seems ugly and grey,
above the clouds it's a beautiful day.'
'So spread your arms and up we go,
soar with me to the rainbow!'

And so Octopus's belief in himself was right,
he was up in the sky, making a flight.
Beneath him everything turned so small,
What a great feeling, flying above this all!

Bird said: 'Octopus, make yourself long,
don't worry I'll catch you, it can't go wrong.'

'And now become a ball,
that'll break the free-fall.'

'Bird', Octopus said, 'I have never,
experienced anything as magnificent as this whatsoever.'
'It is my most exciting day, without a doubt.'
And shortly after Octopus found out:

If you have faith in yourself one hundred percent,
no one can possibly -- not even your best friend --
keep you from what you want to do,
to make all of your wildest dreams come true.
For Octopus it was no longer a surprise,
because today he'd seen with his own eyes:

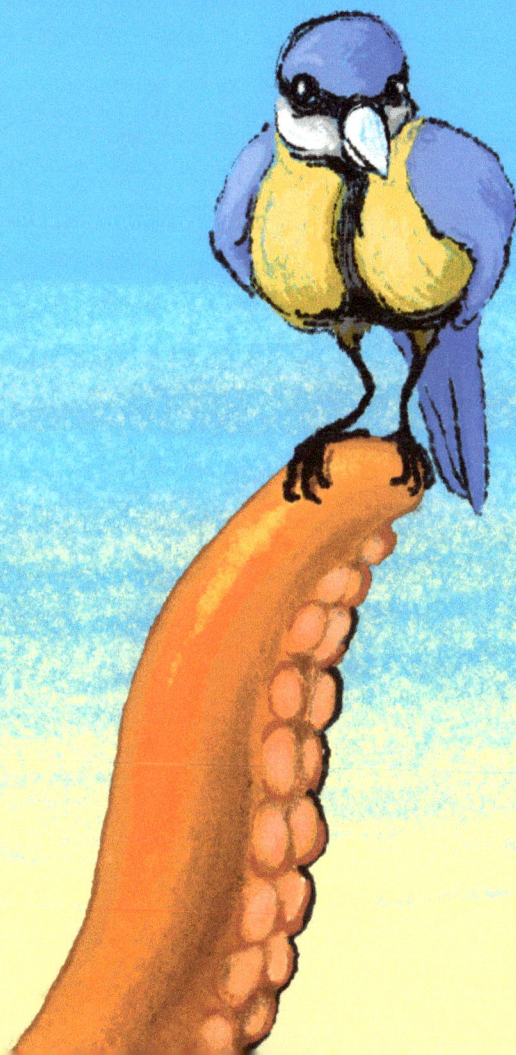

Sometimes it may not seem so bright,
and luck is not on your side,
know then, that when dark clouds appear,
the sun always shines behind them, in a sky perfectly clear.

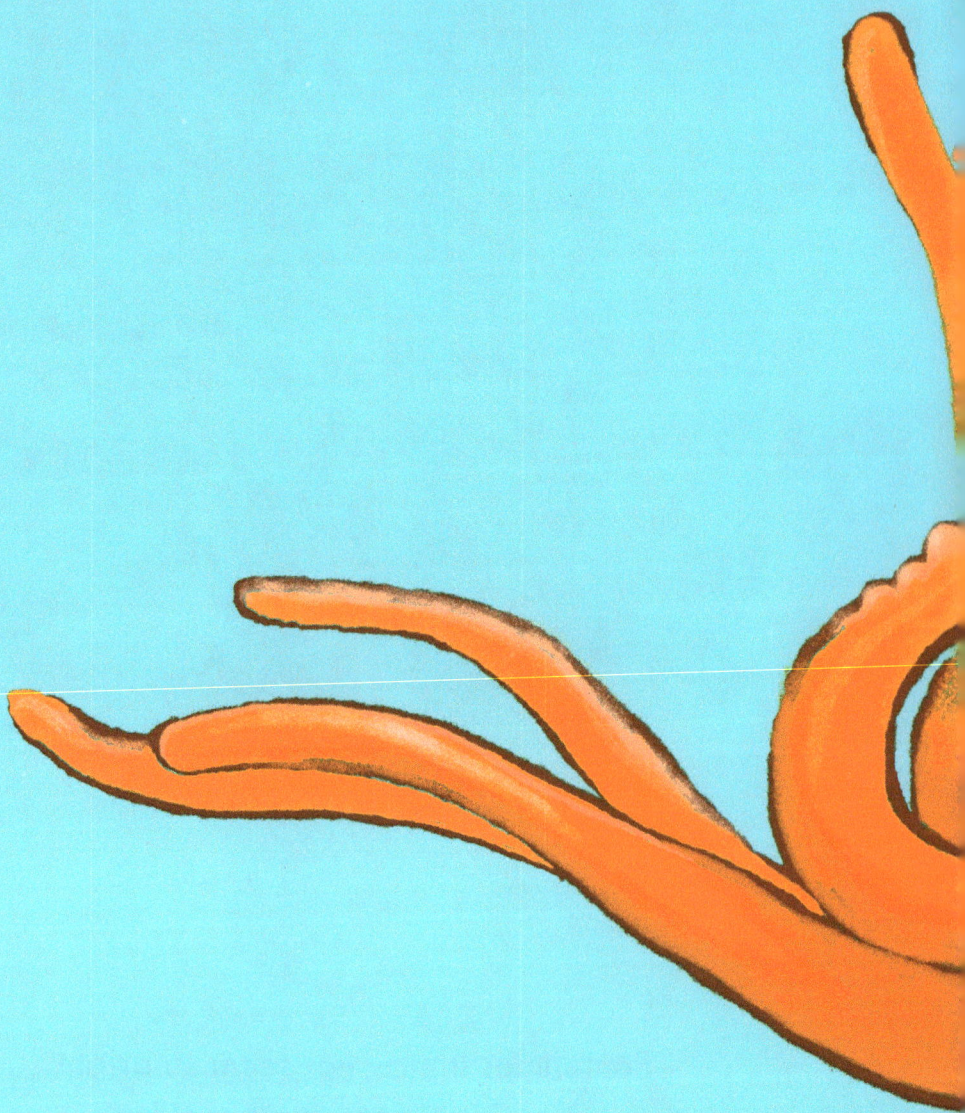

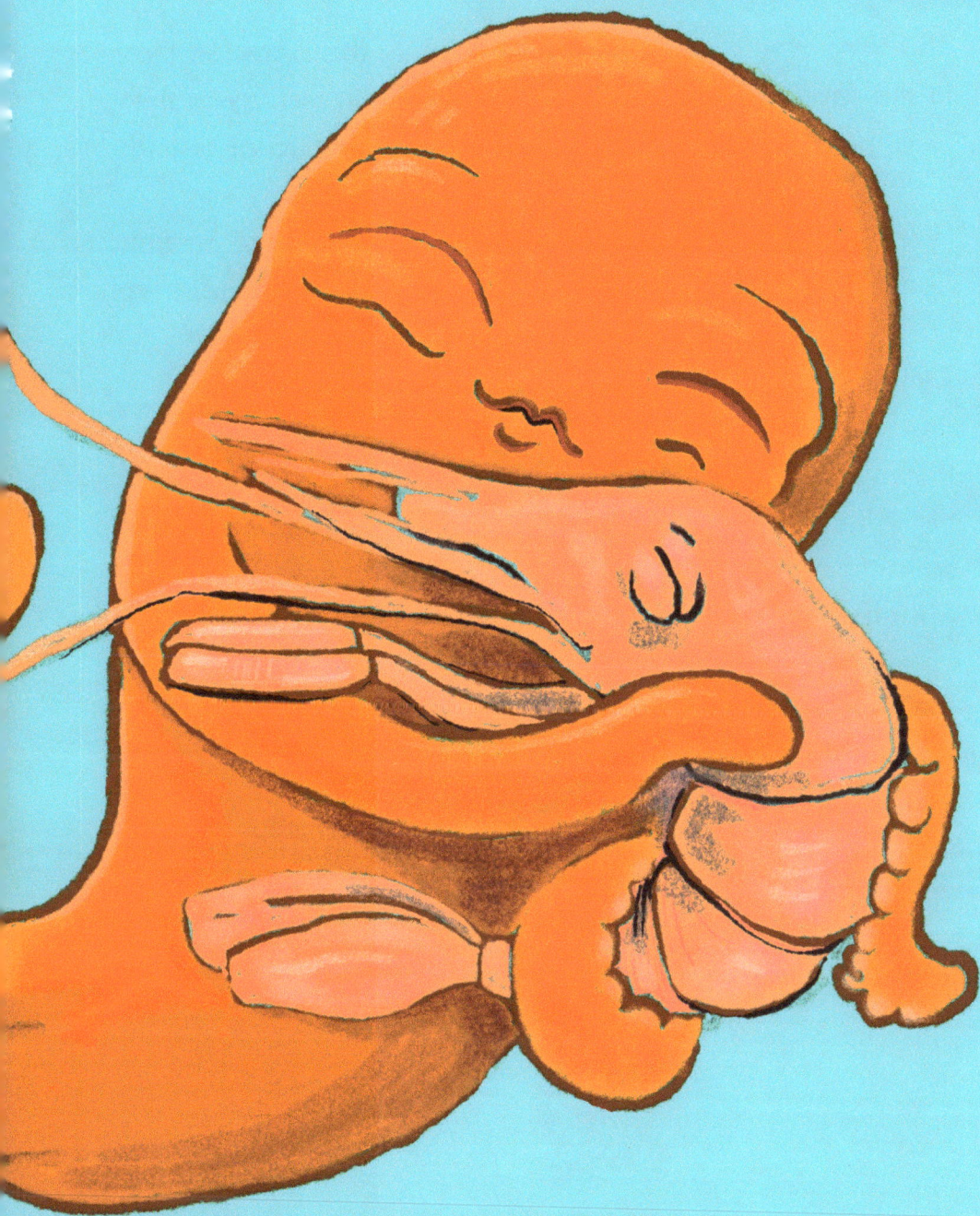

About this book

This is not Octopus's first adventure. In the book, 'A Day in the Mountains', he went running and in 'A Day in the Sea' he showed his friend Horse the underwater world.

'We can do anything we want,' Octopus says to Shrimp. Some things may seem impossible but if you believe you can do it, you can achieve anything you want. That's Octopus's motto in life.

It's important to him to make his dreams come true and he will do whatever it takes to succeed. His idea may seem impossible, but nothing will stop him, not his friend Shrimp, nor the bad weather.

Stepping out of your comfort zone, seeking adventure, and surprising yourself and your loved ones are the main themes in all three books.

www.ingramcontent.com/pod-product-compliance
Lightning Source LLC
Chambersburg PA
CBHW062334150426
42813CB00078B/2806